SIRT FOOD DIET RECIPES FOR BEGINNERS

The Ultimate Guide to the Sirt Food Diet

© Copyright 2021 - All rights reserved.

The content contained within this book may not be reproduced, duplicated or transmitted without direct written permission from the author or the publisher.

Under no circumstances will any blame or legal responsibility be held against the publisher, or author, for any damages, reparation, or monetary loss due to the information contained within this book. Either directly or indirectly.

Legal Notice:

This book is copyright protected. This book is only for personal use. You cannot amend, distribute, sell, use, quote or paraphrase any part, or the content within this book, without the consent of the author or publisher.

Disclaimer Notice:

Please note the information contained within this document is for educational and entertainment purposes only. All effort has been executed to present accurate, up to date, and reliable, complete information. No warranties of any kind are declared or implied. Readers acknowledge that the author is not engaging in the rendering of legal, financial, medical or professional advice. The content within this book has been derived from various sources. Please consult a licensed professional before attempting any techniques outlined in this book.

By reading this document, the reader agrees that under no circumstances is the author responsible for any losses, direct or indirect, which are incurred as a result of the use of information contained within this document, including, but not limited to, — errors, omissions, or inaccuracies.

Sommario

INTRODUCTION 7
   Chapter 1: Breakfast Recipes 9
Strawberry and Cherry Smoothie 9
Eggs with Kale 11
Banana Snap 12
Green Egg Scramble 13
Strawberry Blend 14
Avocado Kale smoothie 14
Green Sirtfood Smoothie 15
Power cereals 17
Berry Yoghurt 19
Yoghurt with berries 20
Blueberry frozen yogurt 21
Vegetable & Nut Loaf 23
Dates & Parma Ham 25
Braised Celery 26
Cheesy Buckwheat Cakes 27
Red Chicory & Stilton Cheese Boats 29
Strawberry, Rocket (Arugula) & Feta Salad 30
Scrambled eggs 31
   Chapter 2: Fluids 33
Beef Broth 33
Tomato Juice 36
Cupcakes with Matcha Icing 37
Green Sirtfood Juice 40
Celery juice with kale and apple 42
Celery juice with pineapple, apple and parsley 43
Matcha tea 44
   Chapter 3: Main Meals 47
Salmon and Capers 47

Coconut curry	49
Tofu Thai Curry	51
Turkey Curry	53
Sirtfood pizza	55
Red Coleslaw	58
Avocado Mayo Medley	60
Amazing Garlic Aioli	62
Easy Seed Crackers	64
Hearty Almond Crackers	67
Black Bean Salsa	69
Corn Spread	71
Moroccan Leeks Snack	73
The Bell Pepper Fiesta	75
Spiced Up Pumpkin Seeds Bowls	77
Mozzarella Cauliflower Bars	79
Chicken curry with potatoes and kale	81
Fruit Skewers & Strawberry Dip	84
Choc Nut Truffles	85
No-Bake Strawberry Flapjacks	86
Chocolate Balls	88
Warm Berries & Cream	90
Chocolate Fondue	92
Walnut & Date Loaf	93
Chocolate Brownies	95
Crème Brûlée	96
Pistachio Fudge	97
Spiced Poached Apples	98
Black Forest Smoothie	99
Creamy Coffee Smoothie	100
Strawberry Buckwheat Tabouleh	101
Chili con carne	103
Pizza	105

Shitake soup with tofu 108

Chicken with walnut pesto and salad 110

Buckwheat noodles with salmon and rocket 112

Salad with salmon and caramelized chicory 114

Turkey meatball skewers 116

Cod with vegetables 118

Chicken Stir-Fry 122

Tuna With Lemon Herb Dressing 124

Kale, Apple & Fennel Soup 126

Lentil Soup 128

Cauliflower & Walnut Soup 130

Celery & Blue Cheese Soup 132

Spicy Squash Soup 133

French Onion Soup 135

   Chapter 4: Salads 137

Kale and Beef salad 137

Arugula salad 140

Tuna, Tomato and Eggs Salad 141

Crude Brownie Bites 142

Potato Salad 143

Chargrilled Beef 145

Mocha Chocolate Mousse 150

Buckwheat Superfood Muesli 152

Exquisite Turmeric Pancakes with Lemon Yogurt Sauce 154

Sirt Chili Con Carne 157

Chickpea, Quinoa and Turmeric Curry Recipe 159

   Chapter 5: Snacks 163

Kale chips 163

Honey nuts 165

Tofu guacamole 166

Watermelon Juice 167

Snack bites 168

- Choc Bites 169
- Berries Banana Smoothie 171
- Grape and Melon Smoothie 172
- Green Tea Smoothie 173
  - Chapter 6: Juice and Cocktails 175
- Sirtfood green juice 175
- Berries juice 177
- Grapefruit blast 178
- Blueberry blend 179
- Sirt Energy Balls 180
- Kale and Blackcurrant Smoothie 181
  - Chapter 7: Desserts 183
- Yogurt nuts and berries 183
- Sirt muesli 185
- Spiced poached apples 187
- Sirt Chocolate brownies 188
- Pistachio fudge 189
  - CONCLUSION 191

INTRODUCTION

Will you want a diet plan that you can not only use to lose weight? You'll want one that you'll find so delicious and so easy to follow that it can become a part of your life. That's why I thought of and wrote this fantastic cookbook, to give you the tools and all the ideal ingredients to make up amazing dishes!!!

Sitfood more than a diet is a lifestyle that will accompany you every day, making you feel satisfied but light.

But let's not get lost in chatter, let's run straight to the kitchen to start this fantastic adventure.

Chapter 1: Breakfast Recipes

Strawberry and Cherry Smoothie

Ingredients

100g (3½ oz) strawberries

75g (3oz) frozen pitted cherries

1 tablespoon plain full-fat yogurt

175mls (6fl oz) unsweetened soya milk

Serves 1

132 calories per serving

Method

Place all of the **Ingredients** into a blender and process until smooth. Serve and enjoy.

Eggs with Kale

Serves 1

Ingredients - Allergies: SF, GF, DF, NF

- 2 large eggs

- S*alt*

- **G**round black pepper

- 1 tsp. olive oil or avocado **oil**

- **1** cup kale

Instructions

Heat 1 tsp. olive oil in the skillet over (medium/high) heat. Add kale and cook, tossing, until wilted (Approx. 1 minute). Remove kale, add eggs and fry until done. Serve with kale.

Banana Snap

Ingredients

2.5cm (1 inch) chunk of fresh ginger, peeled

1 banana

1 large carrot

1 apple, cored

½ stick of celery

¼ level teaspoon turmeric powder

Serves 1

166 calories per serving

Directions:

Place all the **Ingredients** into a blender with just enough water to cover them. Process until smooth

Green Egg Scramble

Ingredients

2 eggs, whisked

25g (1oz) rocket (arugula) leaves

1 teaspoon chives, chopped

1 teaspoon fresh basil, chopped

1 teaspoon fresh parsley, chopped

1 tablespoon olive oil

Serves 1

250 calories per serving

Directions:

Mix the eggs together with the rocket (arugula) and herbs. Heat the oil in a frying pan and pour into the egg mixture. Gently stir until it's lightly scrambled. Season and serve.

Strawberry Blend

Avocado Kale smoothie

3 stalks of kales

1 avocado, peeled & de-stoned

1 teaspoon fresh parsley

½ teaspoon matcha powder

Juice of ½ lemon

Method 306 calories per serving

Place all of the **Ingredients** into a blender and add enough water to cover them. Process until creamy and smooth.

Green Sirtfood Smoothie

We recommend this smoothie recipe especially in your sirtfood diet, because it contains a lot of sirtuin activators

For one serving:

- 100g unsweetened Greek yoghurt
- 6 walnut halves
- 8-10 medium strawberries
- a handful of kale leaves
- 20g dark chocolate (min. 85% cocoa)
- 1 date
- 1/2 teaspoon turmeric
- Small piece fresh chili, finely chopped
- 200ml unsweetened almond milk

If you prefer to eat vegan, use soy yoghurt instead of Greek yoghurt.

Put everything into a blender and mix until you get a smoothie.

Power cereals

For one serving. The ultimate start to the day with extra sirtuin foods.

- 20g buckwheat flakes
- 10g puffed buckwheat
- 15g coconut flakes
- 40g Medjool dates, seeded and chopped
- 10g cocoa nibs
- 100g strawberries
- 100g Greek natural yoghurt

Mix all **Ingredients** together. Done.

If you are preparing on stock, e.g. for five portions, simply take five times the amount. You can store them for a few days in an airtight tin.

If you prefer to eat vegan, use soy yoghurt instead of Greek yoghurt.

Instead of strawberries you can also use other berries, e.g. raspberries, blueberries or blackberries.

Berry Yoghurt

For breakfast as part of your sirtfood diet we suggest this yoghurt for example:

- 125g mixed berries, e.g. blueberries, strawberries and blackberries

- 150g Greek yoghurt

- 25g walnuts, chopped

- 10g dark chocolate (85%), grated

Simply mix all **Ingredients** together.

Vegans can also use soy yoghurt and vegan chocolate instead of yoghurt.

Yoghurt with berries

A wonderful start to the day:

- unsweetened yoghurt (125g)

- fresh berries, e.g. raspberries, approx. 60g.

Raspberries belong to the so-called Sirt foods - and so this breakfast is also suitable as part of a Sirt food diet.

Blueberry frozen yogurt

Ingredients

450g (1lb) plain yogurt

175g (6oz) blueberries

Juice of 1 orange

1 tablespoon honey

Serves 4

133 calories per serving

Directions:

Place the blueberries and orange juice into a food processor or blender and blitz until smooth. Press the mixture through a sieve into a large bowl to remove seeds. Stir in the honey and yogurt. Transfer the mixture to an ice-cream maker and follow the manufacturer's instructions. Alternatively pour the mixture into a container and place in the fridge for 1 hour. Use a fork to whisk it and break up ice crystals and freeze for 2 hours.

Vegetable & Nut Loaf

Ingredients

175g (6oz) mushrooms, finely chopped

100g (3½ oz) haricot beans

100g (3½ oz) walnuts, finely chopped

100g (3½ oz) peanuts, finely chopped

1 carrot, finely chopped

3 sticks celery, finely chopped

1 bird's-eye chilli, finely chopped

1 red onion, finely chopped

1 egg, beaten

2 cloves of garlic, chopped

2 tablespoons olive oil

2 teaspoons turmeric powder

2 tablespoons soy sauce

4 tablespoons fresh parsley, chopped

100mls (3½ fl oz) water

60mls (2fl oz) red wine

Serves 4

453 calories per serving

Directions:

Heat the oil in a pan and add the garlic, chilli, carrot, celery, onion, mushrooms and turmeric. Cook for 5 minutes. Place the haricot beans in a bowl and stir in the nuts, vegetables, soy sauce, egg, parsley, red wine and water. Grease and line a large loaf tin with greaseproof paper. Spoon the mixture into the loaf tin, cover with foil and bake in the oven at 190C/375F for 60-90 minutes. Let it stand for 10 minutes then turn onto a serving plate.

Dates & Parma Ham

Ingredients

12 medjool dates

2 slices of Parma ham, cut into strips

Serves 4

202 calories per serving

Directions:

Wrap each date with a strip of Parma ham. Can be served hot or cold.

Braised Celery

Ingredients

250g (9oz) celery, chopped

100mls (3½ fl oz) warm vegetable stock (broth)

1 red onion, chopped

1 clove of garlic, crushed

1 tablespoon fresh parsley, chopped

25g (1oz) butter

Sea salt and freshly ground black pepper

Serves 4

67 calories per serving

Directions:

Place the celery, onion, stock (broth) and garlic into a saucepan and bring it to the boil, reduce the heat and simmer for 10 minutes. Stir in the parsley and butter and season with salt and pepper. Serve as an accompaniment to roast meat dishes.

Cheesy Buckwheat Cakes

Ingredients

100g (3½oz) buckwheat, cooked and cooled

1 large egg

25g (1oz) cheddar cheese, grated (shredded)

25g (1oz) wholemeal breadcrumbs

2 shallots, chopped

2 tablespoons fresh parsley, chopped

1 tablespoon olive oil

Serves 2

358 calories per serving

Directions:

Crack the egg into a bowl, whisk it then set aside. In a separate bowl combine all the buckwheat, cheese, shallots and parsley and mix well. Pour in the beaten egg to the buckwheat mixture and stir well. Shape the mixture into patties. Scatter the breadcrumbs on a plate and roll the patties in them. Heat the olive oil in a large frying pan and gently place the cakes in the oil. Cook for 3-4 minutes on either side until slightly golden.

Red Chicory & Stilton Cheese Boats

Ingredients

200g (7oz) stilton cheese, crumbled

200g (7oz) red chicory leaves (or if unavailable, use yellow)

2 tablespoon fresh parsley, chopped

1 tablespoon olive oil

Serves 4

250 calories per serving

Directions:

Place the red chicory leaves onto a baking sheet. Drizzle them with olive oil then sprinkle the cheese inside the leaves. Place them under a hot grill (broiler) for around 4 minutes until the cheese has melted. Sprinkle with chopped parsley and serve straight away.

Strawberry, Rocket (Arugula) & Feta Salad

Ingredients

75g (3oz) fresh rocket (arugula) leaves

75g (3oz) feta cheese, crumbled

100g (3½ oz) strawberries, halved

8 walnut halves

2 tablespoons flaxseeds

Serves 2

268 calories per serving

Directions:

Combine all the **Ingredients** in a bowl then scatter them onto two plates. For an extra Sirt food boost you can drizzle over some olive oil.

Scrambled eggs

For one serving:

- 1 teaspoon of extra virgin olive oil
- 20g red onions, finely chopped
- 1/2 red chili, finely chopped
- 3 medium-sized organic eggs
- 50ml milk
- 1 teaspoon turmeric
- 5g parsley, finely chopped

Heat the olive oil in a coated pan and sauté the onion in it, it should not brown.

Mix the egg, milk, chili, turmeric and parsley in a bowl with a fork to a uniform mixture and add to the pan. Let it boil to the desired consistency while stirring regularly.

Chapter 2: Fluids

Beef Broth

Ingredients

- 4-5 pounds beef bones and few veal bones

- 1 pound of stew meat (chuck or flank steak) cut into 2-inch chunks

- <u>olive</u> oil

- 1-2 medium red onions, peeled and quartered

- 1-2 large carrots, cut into 1-2 inch segments

- 1 celery rib, cut into 1 inch segments

- 2-3 cloves of garlic, unpeeled

- Handful of parsley, stems and leaves

- 1-2 bay leaves

- 10 peppercorns

Instructions - Allergies: SF, GF, DF, EF, NF

Heat oven to 375°F. Rub olive oil over the stew meat pieces, carrots, and onions. Place stew meat or beef scraps, stock bones, carrots and onions in a large roasting pan. Roast in oven for about 45 minutes, turning everything half-way through the cooking.

Place everything from the oven in a large stock pot. Pour some boiling water in the oven pan and scrape up all of the browned bits and pour all in the stock pot.

Add parsley, celery, garlic, bay leaves, and peppercorns to the pot. Fill the pot with cold water, to 1 inch over the top of the bones.

Bring the stock pot to a regular simmer and then reduce the heat to low, so it just barely simmers. Cover the pot loosely and let simmer low and slow for 3-4 hours.

Scoop away the fat and any scum that rises to the surface once in a while.

After cooking, remove the bones and vegetables from the pot. Strain the broth. Let cool to room temperature and then put in the refrigerator.

The fat will solidify once the broth has chilled. Discard the fat (or reuse it) and pour the broth into a jar and freeze it.

Tomato Juice

Ingredients

- 5 lbs. chopped plum tomatoes
- 1/4 cup extra-virgin olive oil plus 2 tbsp.
- salt, to taste

Instructions - Allergies: SF, GF, DF, EF, V, NF

Heat 1/4 cup of the oil in a skillet over (medium/high) heat. Add tomatoes. Season with salt. Bring to a boil. Cook, stirring, until very soft, about 8 minutes.

Pass the tomatoes through the finest plate of a food mill. Push as much of the pulp through the sieve as possible and leave the seeds behind. Bring it to boil, lower it and then boil uncovered, so the liquid will thicken (approx. 30-40 minutes).

Cupcakes with Matcha Icing

Makes 12

Ingredients

½ teaspoon of salt

200g of caster sugar

½ teaspoon of vanilla extract

150g of self-rising flour

60g of cocoa

1 egg

120ml milk

½ teaspoon of fine espresso coffee, decaf if preferred

120ml of boiling water

50ml of vegetable oil

For the icing

1 tablespoon of matcha green tea powder

50g of at room temperature butter

50g of icing sugar

½ teaspoon of vanilla bean paste

50g of soft cream cheese

Instructions

1. Heat the oven to 180C or 160C fan. Line a cupcake tin with silicone cake cases or paper. Thoroughly mix salt, flour, cocoa, sugar, and espresso powder in a large bowl.

2. Add the milk, vegetable oil, vanilla extract, and egg to the other **Ingredients** and beat them well using an electric mixer.

3. Carefully pour boiling water into the electric mixer and mix on low speed until perfectly combined. Mix on high for about a minute to add some air into the batter. The batter will appear liquid than what you would expect for normal cakes; this is how it should be.

4. Evenly add the batter into the cake cases no more than ¾ full. Place them into the preheated oven and bake for about 15-18 minutes or until the mixture can bounce back when tapped.

5. When done, remove from the oven and allow them to cool before icing.

6. For the icing, mix the icing sugar and the butter until pale and smooth. Add matcha powder mixed with vanilla and stir well again. Finally, add the cream cheese and mix until smooth. Spread this mixture over the cakes and serve.

Green Sirtfood Juice

For about 300ml. The ultimate sirtfood juice with many sirtuin foods. You will need a juicer for this.

2 large handfuls of kale

1 large handful of rocket salad

1 very small hand flat parsley

1 very small hand lovage leaves

2 to 3 sticks of celery, with leaves

1/2 small green apple, e.g. Granny Smith

½ Organic lemon with peel

1/2 teaspoon Matcha powder

First put the kale, rocket, parsley and lovage into the juicer.

Then juice the apple, the celery stalks and half the lemon.

This should give about 300ml of juice.

Finally dissolve the Matcha powder in the juice and the Sirtfood juice is ready.

Celery juice with kale and apple

For about 500ml. You will need a juicer for this.

300 g celery

200 g cucumbers

50 g kale, without stalk

70 g apple (1/2 apple with skin)

1/2 organic lemon with peel

5 g ginger with peel

Wash all **Ingredients** well and cut them to fit the feed chute of the juicer.

Then gradually pour into the feed chute and allow to press out.

If you prepare more juice in stock, the juice will last one or two days in the refrigerator.

Celery juice with pineapple, apple and parsley

For about 400ml. You will need a juicer for this.

300 g celery approx. half a perennial

180 g pineapple peeled

20 g parsley

70 g apple (1/2 apple with skin)

1/2 organic lemon with peel

Wash all **Ingredients** well and cut them to fit the feed chute of the juicer.

Then gradually pour into the feed chute and allow to press out.

If you prepare more juice in stock, the juice will last one or two days in the refrigerator.

Matcha tea

Matcha is a finely ground green tea. Its particularly intense colour is obtained by protecting the plant from the sun for about 4 weeks before harvesting: It then only grows in the shade. This allows much of the green colour chlorophyll and good amino acids (for a mild taste) to be formed.

Indeed, regular consumption of Matcha tea can contribute to weight loss as numerous studies have shown. The catechins contained have a positive effect on the burning of fat and promote the metabolism.

Especially recommended are all Matcha teas from Japan. The best is fair trade and organic farming.

Matcha tea preparation - classic with water

You can prepare your Matcha tea very easily.

Put 1 level teaspoon of Matcha powder in a bowl. You can also use a special bamboo Matcha spoon to dose the powder: Its name is "Chakasu".

Pour about 50 ml of water over the powder. The water should be 80 degrees warm - not hotter, otherwise valuable **Ingredients** are killed.

Then mix everything with the Matcha broom until it is frothy. You can add more water depending on the desired taste. Just try out how you like the Matcha tea best.

Chapter 3: Main Meals

Salmon and Capers

Ingredients

75g (3oz) Greek yogurt

4 salmon fillets, skin removed

4 teaspoons Dijon Mustard

1 tablespoon capers, chopped

2 teaspoons fresh parsley

Zest of 1 lemon

Serves 4

321 calories per serving

Method

In a bowl, mix together the yogurt, mustard, lemon zest, parsley and capers. Thoroughly coat the salmon in the mixture. Place the salmon under a hot grill (broiler) and cook for 3-4 minutes on each side, or until the fish is cooked. Serve with mashed potatoes and vegetables or a large green leafy salad.

Coconut curry

Ingredients

400g (14oz) tinned chopped tomatoes

25g (1oz) fresh coriander (cilantro) chopped

3 red onions, finely chopped

3 cloves of garlic, crushed

2 bird's eye chillies

½ teaspoon ground coriander (cilantro)

½ teaspoon turmeric

400mls (14fl oz) coconut milk

1 tablespoons olive oil

Juice of 1 lime

Serves 4

322 calories per serving

Method

Place the onions, garlic, tomatoes, chillies, lime juice, turmeric, ground coriander (cilantro), chillies and half of the fresh coriander (cilantro) into a blender and blitz until you have a smooth curry paste. Heat the olive oil in a frying pan, add the paste and cook for 2 minutes. Stir in the coconut milk and warm it thoroughly. Stir in the fresh coriander (cilantro). Serve with rice

Tofu Thai Curry

Serves 4

Ingredients

400g (14oz) tofu, diced

200g (7oz) sugar snap peas

5cm (2 inch) chunk fresh ginger root, peeled and finely chopped

2 red onions, chopped

2 cloves of garlic, crushed

2 bird's eye chillies

2 tablespoons tomato puree

1 stalk of lemon grass, inner stalks only

1 tablespoon fresh coriander (cilantro), chopped

1 teaspoon cumin

300mls (½ pint) coconut milk

200mls (7fl oz) vegetable stock (broth)

1 tablespoon virgin olive oil

Juice of 1 lime

Serves 4

270 calories per serving

Method

Heat the oil in a frying pan, add the onion and cook for 4 minutes. Add in the chillies, cumin, ginger, and garlic and cook for 2 minutes. Add the tomato puree, lemon grass, sugar-snap peas, lime juice and tofu and cook for 2 minutes. Pour in the stock (broth), coconut milk and coriander (cilantro) and simmer for 5 minutes. Serve with brown rice or buckwheat and a handful of rocket (arugula) leaves on the side.

Turkey Curry

Ingredients

450g (1lb) turkey breasts, chopped

100g (3½ oz) fresh rocket (arugula) leaves

5 cloves garlic, chopped

3 teaspoons medium curry powder

2 teaspoons turmeric powder

2 tablespoons fresh coriander (cilantro), finely chopped

2 bird's-eye chillies, chopped

2 red onions, chopped

400mls (14fl oz) full-fat coconut milk

2 tablespoons olive oil

Serves 4

402 calories per serving

Method

Heat the olive oil in a saucepan, add the chopped red onions and cook them for around 5 minutes or until soft. Stir in the garlic and the turkey and cook it for 7-8 minutes. Stir in the turmeric, chillies and curry powder then add the coconut milk and coriander (cilantro). Bring it to the boil, reduce the heat and simmer for around 10 minutes. Scatter the rocket (arugula) onto plates and spoon the curry on top. Serve alongside brown rice.

Sirtfood pizza

For the dough

7g dry yeast

1 teaspoon brown sugar

300ml water

200g buckwheat flour

200g wheat flour for pasta

1 tablespoon of olive oil

Dissolve dry yeast and sugar in water and leave covered for 15 minutes. Then mix the flours. Add the yeast water and oil and make a dough.

Preheat oven to 425 °. Then knead the dough well again and form two pizzas, each 30 cm in diameter, with a rolling pin on a floured work surface. Or you can form a thin pizza that fits on a whole baking sheet.

Spread the pizza dough on a baking tray lined with baking paper.

For the sauce

1/2 red onion, finely chopped

1 clove of garlic, finely chopped

1 teaspoon of olive oil

1 teaspoon oregano, dried

2 tablespoons red wine

1 can of strained tomatoes (400ml)

1 pinch of brown sugar

5g basil leaves

Fry the garlic, onion and sugar with olive oil, add the wine and oregano and cook briefly. Then add the tomatoes and cook on low heat for 30 minutes. Then set aside and add the fresh basil leaves.

Pizza topping and baking

Spread the desired amount of tomato sauce on the dough - leave the edges as free as possible, do not spread too thickly.

Then add the desired **Ingredients**, for example

sliced red onion and grilled eggplant

Goat cheese and cherry tomatoes

Chicken breast (grilled), red onions and olives

Kale, chorizo and red onions

Then bake for about 12 minutes and, if desired, sprinkle with rocket, pepper and chili flakes.

Red Coleslaw

Serving: 4
Preparation time: 10 minutes
Cook Time: 0 minutes

Ingredients:

1 2/3 pounds red cabbage

2 tablespoons ground caraway seeds

1 tablespoon whole grain mustard

1 1/4 cups mayonnaise, low fat, low sodium

Salt and black pepper

How To:

Cut the red cabbage into small slices.

Take a large-sized bowl and add all the **Ingredients** alongside cabbage.

Mix well, season with salt and pepper.

Serve and enjoy! [F19]

Nutrition (Per Serving)

Calories: 406

Fat: 40.8g

Carbohydrates: 10g

Protein: 2.2g

Avocado Mayo Medley

Serving: 4

Preparation time: 5 minutes

Cook Time: Nil

Ingredients:

1 medium avocado, cut into chunks

½ teaspoon ground cayenne pepper

2 tablespoons fresh cilantro

¼ cup olive oil

½ cup mayo, low fat and los sodium

How To:

Take a food processor and add avocado, cayenne pepper, lime juice, salt and cilantro.

Mix until smooth.

Slowly incorporate olive oil, add 1 tablespoon at a time and keep processing between additions.

Store and use as needed!

Nutrition (Per Serving)

Calories: 231

Fat: 20g

Carbohydrates: 5g

Protein: 3g

Amazing Garlic Aioli

Serving: 4

Preparation time: 5 minutes

Cook Time: Nil

Ingredients:

½ cup mayonnaise, low fat and low sodium

2 garlic cloves, minced

Juice of 1 lemon

1 tablespoon fresh-flat leaf Italian parsley, chopped

1 teaspoon chives, chopped

Salt and pepper to taste

How To:

Add mayonnaise, garlic, parsley, lemon juice, chives and season with salt and pepper.

Blend until combined well.

Pour into refrigerator and chill for 30 minutes.

Serve and use as needed!

Nutrition (Per Serving)

Calories: 813

Fat: 88g

Carbohydrates: 9g

Protein: 2g

Easy Seed Crackers

Serving: 72 crackers

Preparation time: 10 minutes

Cooking Time: 60 minutes

Ingredients:

1 cup boiling water

1/3 cup chia seeds

1/3 cup sesame seeds

1/3 cup pumpkin seeds

1/3 cup Flaxseeds

1/3 cup sunflower seeds

1 tablespoon Psyllium powder

1 cup almond flour

1 teaspoon salt

¼ cup coconut oil, melted

How To:

Pre-heat your oven to 300 degrees F.

Line a cookie sheet with parchment paper and keep it on the side.

Add listed **Ingredients** (except coconut oil and water) to food processor and pulse until ground.

Transfer to a large mixing bowl and pour melted coconut oil and boiling water, mix.

Transfer mix to prepared sheet and spread into a thin layer.

Cut dough into crackers and bake for 60 minutes.

Cool and serve.

Enjoy!

Nutrition (Per Serving)

Total Carbs: 10.6g

Fiber: 3g

Protein: 5g

Fat: 14.6g

Hearty Almond Crackers

> **Serving: 40 crackers**
>
> **Preparation time: 10 minutes**
>
> **Cooking Time: 20 minutes**

Ingredients:

1 cup almond flour

¼ teaspoon baking soda

1/8 teaspoon black pepper

3 tablespoons sesame seeds

1 egg, beaten

Salt and pepper to taste

How To:

Pre-heat your oven to 350 degrees F.

Line two baking sheets with parchment paper and keep them on the side.

Mix the dry **Ingredients** in a large bowl and add egg, mix well and form dough.

Divide dough into two balls.

Roll out the dough between two pieces of parchment paper.

Cut into crackers and transfer them to prepared baking sheet.

Bake for 15-20 minutes.

Repeat until all the dough has been used up.

Leave crackers to cool and serve.

Enjoy!

Nutrition (Per Serving)

Total Carbs: 8g

Fiber: 2g

Protein: 9g

Fat: 28g

Black Bean Salsa

Serving: 4

Preparation time: 10 minutes

Cook Time: Nil

Ingredients:

1 tablespoon coconut aminos

½ teaspoon cumin, ground

1 cup canned black beans, no salt

1 cup salsa

6 cups romaine lettuce, torn

½ cup avocado, peeled, pitted and cubed

How To:

Take a bowl and add beans, alongside other **Ingredients**.

Toss well and serve.

Enjoy!

Nutrition (Per Serving)

Calories: 181

Fat: 5g

Carbohydrates: 14g

Protein: 7g

Corn Spread

Serving: 4
Preparation time: 10 minutes
Cook Time: 10 minutes

Ingredients:

30 ounce canned corn, drained

2 green onions, chopped

½ cup coconut cream

1 jalapeno, chopped

½ teaspoon chili powder

How To:

Take a pan and add corn, green onions, jalapeno, chili powder, stir well.

Bring to a simmer over medium heat and cook for 10 minutes.

Let it chill and add coconut cream.

Stir well.

Serve and enjoy!

Nutrition (Per Serving)

Calories: 192

Fat: 5g

Carbohydrates: 11g

Protein: 8g

Moroccan Leeks Snack

Serving: 4

Preparation time: 10 minutes

Cook Time: nil

Ingredients:

1 bunch radish, sliced

3 cups leeks, chopped

1 ½ cups olives, pitted and sliced

Pinch turmeric powder

2 tablespoons essential olive oil

1 cup cilantro, chopped

How To:

Take a bowl and mix in radishes, leeks, olives and cilantro.

Mix well.

Season with pepper, oil, turmeric and toss well.

Serve and enjoy!

Nutrition (Per Serving)

Calories: 120

Fat: 1g

Carbohydrates: 1g

Protein: 6g

The Bell Pepper Fiesta

Serving: 4

Preparation time: 10 minutes

Cook Time: nil

Ingredients:

2 tablespoons dill, chopped

1 yellow onion, chopped

1 pound multi colored peppers, cut, halved, seeded and cut into thin strips

3 tablespoons organic olive oil

2 ½ tablespoons white wine vinegar

Black pepper to taste

How To:

Take a bowl and mix in sweet pepper, onion, dill, pepper, oil, vinegar and toss well.

Divide between bowls and serve.

Enjoy!

Nutrition (Per Serving)

Calories: 120

Fat: 3g

Carbohydrates: 1g

Protein: 6g

Spiced Up Pumpkin Seeds Bowls

Serving: 4

Preparation time: 10 minutes

Cook Time: 20 minutes

Ingredients:

½ tablespoon chili powder

½ teaspoon cayenne

2 cups pumpkin seeds

2 teaspoons lime juice

How To:

Spread pumpkin seeds over lined baking sheet, add lime juice, cayenne and chili powder.

Toss well.

Pre-heat your oven to 275 degrees F.

Roast in your oven for 20 minutes and transfer to small bowls.

Serve and enjoy!

Nutrition (Per Serving)

Calories: 170

Fat: 3g

Carbohydrates: 10g

Protein: 6g

Mozzarella Cauliflower Bars

Serving: 4

Preparation time: 10 minutes

Cook Time: 40 minutes

Ingredients:

1 cauliflower head, riced

12 cup low-fat mozzarella cheese, shredded

¼ cup egg whites

1 teaspoon Italian dressing, low fat

Pepper to taste

How To:

Spread cauliflower rice over lined baking sheet.

Pre-heat your oven to 375 degrees F.

Roast for 20 minutes.

Transfer to bowl and spread pepper, cheese, seasoning, egg whites and stir well.

Spread in a rectangular pan and press.

Transfer to oven and cook for 20 minutes more.

Serve and enjoy!

Nutrition (Per Serving)

Calories: 140

Fat: 2g

Carbohydrates: 6g

Protein: 6g

Chicken curry with potatoes and kale

For four servings:

600g chicken breast, cut into pieces

4 tablespoons of extra virgin olive oil

3 tablespoons turmeric

2 red onions, sliced

2 red chilies, finely chopped

3 cloves of garlic, finely chopped

1 tablespoon freshly chopped ginger

1 tablespoon curry powder

1 tin of small tomatoes (400ml)

500ml chicken broth

200ml coconut milk

2 pieces cardamom

1 cinnamon stick

600g potatoes (mainly waxy)

10g parsley, chopped

175g kale, chopped

5g coriander, chopped

Marinate the chicken in a teaspoon of olive oil and a tablespoon of turmeric for about 30 minutes. Then fry in a high frying pan at high heat for about 4 minutes. Remove from the pan and set aside.

Heat a tablespoon of oil in a pan with chili, garlic, onion and ginger. Boil everything over medium heat and then add the curry powder and a tablespoon of turmeric and cook for another two minutes, stirring occasionally. Add tomatoes, cook for another two minutes until finally chicken stock, coconut milk, cardamom and cinnamon stick are added. Cook for about 45 to 60 minutes and add some broth if necessary.

In the meantime, preheat the oven to 425 °. Peel and chop the potatoes. Bring water to the boil, add the potatoes with turmeric and cook for 5 minutes. Then pour off the water and let it evaporate for about 10 minutes. Spread olive oil together with the potatoes on a baking tray and bake in the oven for 30 minutes.

When the potatoes and curry are almost ready, add the coriander, kale and chicken and cook for five minutes until the chicken is hot.

Add parsley to the potatoes and serve with the chicken curry.

Fruit Skewers & Strawberry Dip

Ingredients

150g (5oz) red grapes

1 pineapple, (approx 2lb weight) peeled and diced

400g (14oz) strawberries

Serves 4

147 calories per serving

Directions:

Place 100g (3½ oz) of the strawberries into a food processor and blend until smooth. Pour the dip into a serving bowl. Skewer the grapes, pineapple chunks and remaining strawberries onto skewers. Serve alongside the strawberry dip.

Choc Nut Truffles

Ingredients

150g (5oz) desiccated (shredded) coconut

50g (2oz) walnuts, chopped

25g (1oz) hazelnuts, chopped

4 medjool dates

2 tablespoons 100% cocoa powder or cacao nibs

1 tablespoon coconut oil

Makes 8

236 calories per serving

Directions:

Place all of the **Ingredients** into a blender and process until smooth and creamy. Using a teaspoon, scoop the mixture into bite-size pieces then roll it into balls. Place them into small paper cases, cover them and chill for 1 hour before serving.

No-Bake Strawberry Flapjacks

Ingredients

75g (3oz) porridge oats

125g (4oz) dates

50g (2oz) strawberries

50g (2oz) peanuts (unsalted)

50g (2oz) walnuts

1 tablespoon coconut oil

2 tablespoons 100% cocoa powder or cacao nibs

Makes 8

182 calories each

Directions:

Place all of the **Ingredients** into a blender and process until they become a soft consistency. Spread the mixture onto a baking sheet or small flat tin. Press the mixture down and smooth it out. Cut it into 8 pieces, ready to serve. You can add an extra sprinkling of cocoa powder to garnish if you wish.

Chocolate Balls

Ingredients

50g (2oz) peanut butter (or almond butter)

25g (1oz) cocoa powder

25g (1oz) desiccated (shredded) coconut

1 tablespoon honey

1 tablespoon cocoa powder for coating

Makes 6 balls

115 calories per serving

Directions:

Place the **Ingredients** into a bowl and mix. Using a teaspoon scoop out a little of the mixture and shape it into a ball. Roll the ball in a little cocoa powder and set aside. Repeat for the remaining mixture. Can be eaten straight away or stored in the fridge.

Warm Berries & Cream

Ingredients

250g (9oz) blueberries

250g (9oz) strawberries

100g (3½ oz) redcurrants

100g (3½ oz) blackberries

4 tablespoons fresh whipped cream

1 tablespoon honey

Zest and juice of 1 orange

Serves 4

180 calories per serving

Directions:

Place all of the berries into a pan along with the honey and orange juice. Gently heat the berries for around 5 minutes until warmed through. Serve the berries into bowls and add a dollop of whipped cream on top. Alternatively you could top them off with fromage frais or yogurt.

Chocolate Fondue

Ingredients

125g (4oz) dark chocolate (min 85% cocoa)

300g (11oz) strawberries

200g (7oz) cherries

2 apples, peeled, cored and sliced

100mls (3½ fl oz) double cream (heavy cream)

Serves 4

352 calories per serving

Directions:

Place the chocolate and cream into a fondue pot or saucepan and warm it until smooth and creamy. Serve in the fondue pot or transfer it to a serving bowl. Scatter the fruit on a serving dish ready to be dipped into the chocolate.

Walnut & Date Loaf

Ingredients

250g (9oz) self-raising flour

125g (4oz) medjool dates, chopped

50g (2oz) walnuts, chopped

250mls (8fl oz) milk

3 eggs

1 medium banana, mashed

1 teaspoon baking soda

Serves 12

166 calories per serving

Directions:

Sieve the baking soda and flour into a bowl. Add in the banana, eggs, milk and dates and combine all the **Ingredients** thoroughly. Transfer the mixture to a lined loaf tin and smooth it out. Scatter the walnuts on top. Bake the loaf in the oven at

180C/360F for 45 minutes. Transfer it to a wire rack to cool before serving.

Chocolate Brownies

Ingredients

200g (7oz) dark chocolate (min 85% cocoa)

200g (7oz) medjool dates, stone removed

100g (3½oz) walnuts, chopped

3 eggs

25mls (1fl oz) melted coconut oil

2 teaspoons vanilla essence

½ teaspoon baking soda

Makes 14   197 calories per serving

Directions:

Place the dates, chocolate, eggs, coconut oil, baking soda and vanilla essence into a food processor and mix until smooth. Stir the walnuts into the mixture. Pour the mixture into a shallow baking tray. Transfer to the oven and bake at 180C/350F for 25-30 minutes. Allow it to cool. Cut into pieces and serve.

Crème Brûlée

Ingredients

400g (14oz) strawberries

300g (11oz) plain low fat yogurt

125g (4oz) Greek yogurt

100g (3½oz) brown sugar

1 teaspoon vanilla extract

Serves 4

213 calories per serving

Directions:

Divide the strawberries between 4 ramekin dishes. In a bowl combine the plain yogurt with the vanilla extract. Spoon the mixture onto the strawberries. Scoop the Greek yogurt on top. Sprinkle the sugar into each ramekin dish, completely covering the top. Place the dishes under a hot grill (broiler) for around 3 minutes or until the sugar has caramelised.

Pistachio Fudge

Ingredients

225g (8oz) medjool dates

100g (3½ oz) pistachio nuts, shelled (or other nuts)

50g (2oz) desiccated (shredded) coconut

25g (1oz) oats

2 tablespoons water

Serves 10

162 calories per serving

Directions:

Place the dates, nuts, coconut, oats and water into a food processor and process until the **Ingredients** are well mixed. Remove the mixture and roll it to 2cm (1 inch) thick. Cut it into 10 pieces and serve.

Spiced Poached Apples

Ingredients

4 apples

2 tablespoons honey

4 star anise

2 cinnamon sticks

300mls (½ pint) green tea

Serves 4

99 calories per serving

Directions:

Place the honey and green tea into a saucepan and bring to the boil. Add the apples, star anise and cinnamon. Reduce the heat and simmer gently for 15 minutes. Serve the apples with a dollop of crème fraiche or Greek yogurt.

Black Forest Smoothie

Ingredients

100g (3½oz) frozen cherries

25g (1oz) kale

1 medjool date

1 tablespoon cocoa powder

2 teaspoons chia seeds

200mls (7fl oz) milk or soya milk

Serves 1

337 calories per serving

Directions:

Place all the **Ingredients** into a blender and process until smooth and creamy.

Creamy Coffee Smoothie

Ingredients

1 banana

1 teaspoon chia seeds

1 teaspoon coffee

½ avocado

120mls (4fl oz) water

Serves 1

239 calories per serving

Directions:

Place all the **Ingredients** into a food processor or blender and blitz until smooth. You can add a little crushed ice too. This can also double as a breakfast smoothie.

Strawberry Buckwheat Tabouleh

Ingredients

50g buckwheat

1 tablespoon turmeric

80g avocado

65g tomatoes

20 g red onion

25 g dates, pitted

1 tablespoon capers

30g parsley

100g strawberries

1 tablespoon of olive oil

Juice of 1/2 lemon

30g rocket salad

Boil the buckwheat together with turmeric and let it cool down.

Finely chop the avocado, tomatoes, red onions, dates, capers and parsley and mix with the cooled buckwheat. Cut the strawberries and mix with the rest. Season with oil and lemon juice. Serve on the rocket.

Chili con carne

Ingredients

1 red onion, chopped

3 cloves of garlic, finely chopped

2 Tai chilies, finely chopped

1 tablespoon of olive oil

1 tablespoon turmeric

1 tablespoon cumin

400g minced beef

150ml red wine

1 red pepper, seeded and diced

2 cans of small tomatoes (400ml each)

1 tablespoon of tomato paste

1 tablespoon cocoa powder (without sugar)

150g canned kidney beans, drained

300ml beef broth

5g coriander green, chopped

5g parsley, chopped

160g buckwheat

Sauté the onions, garlic and chilies in olive oil in a high frying pan or in a frying pan at medium heat. After three minutes add cumin and turmeric and stir.

Then add the minced meat and fry until everything is brown. Add the red wine, bring to the boil and reduce by half.

Add the peppers, tomatoes, tomato paste, cocoa, kidney beans and stock, stir and cook for an hour. Add a little water or broth if the chili is too dry.

Cook buckwheat according to the instructions on the packet and serve sprinkled with the chilies and fresh herbs.

Pizza

For the dough

7g dry yeast

1 teaspoon brown sugar

300ml water

200g buckwheat flour

200g wheat flour for pasta

1 tablespoon of olive oil

Dissolve dry yeast and sugar in water and leave covered for 15 minutes. Then mix the flours. Add the yeast water and oil and make a dough.

Preheat oven to 425 °. Then knead the dough well again and form two pizzas, each 30 cm in diameter, with a rolling pin on a floured work surface. Or you can form a thin pizza that fits on a whole baking sheet.

Spread the pizza dough on a baking tray lined with baking paper.

For the sauce

1/2 red onion, finely chopped

1 clove of garlic, finely chopped

1 teaspoon of olive oil

1 teaspoon oregano, dried

2 tablespoons red wine

1 can of strained tomatoes (400ml)

1 pinch of brown sugar

5g basil leaves

Fry the garlic, onion and sugar with olive oil, add the wine and oregano and cook briefly. Then add the tomatoes and cook on low heat for 30 minutes. Then set aside and add the fresh basil leaves.

Pizza topping and baking

Spread the desired amount of tomato sauce on the dough - leave the edges as free as possible, do not spread too thickly.

Then add the desired **Ingredients**, for example

sliced red onion and grilled eggplant

Goat cheese and cherry tomatoes

Chicken breast (grilled), red onions and olives

Kale, chorizo and red onions

Then bake for about 12 minutes and, if desired, sprinkle with rocket, pepper and chili flakes.

Shitake soup with tofu

10g dried Wakame algae (instant)

1 liter vegetable stock

200g shitake mushrooms, sliced

120g miso paste

400g natural tofu, cut into cubes

2 spring onions

1 red chili, chopped

Bring the stock to boil, add the mushrooms and cook for 2 minutes. In the meantime, dissolve the miso paste in a bowl with some warm stock, put it back into the pot together with the tofu, do not let it boil anymore. Soak the Wakame as needed (on the packet) and add the spring onions and Tai Chi, stir again and serve.

Chicken with walnut pesto and salad

15g parsley

15g walnuts

15g Parmesan cheese

1 tablespoon of extra virgin olive oil

juice of half a lemon

50ml water

150g chicken breast fillet

20g red onions, cut into strips

1 teaspoon red wine vinegar

35g rocket salad

100g cherry tomatoes, halved

1 teaspoon balsamic vinegar

For the pesto, place parsley, walnuts, parmesan, olive oil, half of the lemon juice and a little water in a blender and mix to a paste.

Marinate the chicken in a tablespoon of pesto and the remaining lemon juice for at least 30 minutes.

Preheat oven to 400 °.

Marinate the onions in red wine vinegar for 10 minutes, then drain the liquid.

In the meantime, fry the chicken in a coated pan on both sides at medium heat and place in the preheated oven for 12 minutes.

Remove the chicken from the oven, pour another tablespoon of pesto over it and let it rest for 5 minutes.

Mix the rocket, tomatoes, onions and balsamic vinegar, place the chicken on top and pour the rest of the pesto over it.

Buckwheat noodles with salmon and rocket

For four servings:

2 tablespoons of extra virgin olive oil

1 red onion, finely chopped

2 cloves of garlic, finely chopped

2 red chilies, finely chopped

150g cherry tomatoes, halved

100ml white wine

300g buckwheat noodles

250g smoked salmon

2 tablespoons of capers

juice of half a lemon

60g rocket salad

10g parsley, chopped

Heat 1 teaspoon of the oil in a coated pan, add onions, garlic and chili at medium temperature and fry briefly. Then add the tomatoes and the white wine to the pan and allow the wine to reduce.

Cook the pasta according to the instructions.

In the meantime, cut the salmon into strips and when the pasta is ready, add it to the pan together with the capers, lemon juice, capers rocket, remaining olive oil and parsley and mix. Done.

Salad with salmon and caramelized chicory

For one serving:

10g parsley

juice of a quarter of a lemon

1 tablespoon capers

extra virgin olive oil

1/4 avocado sliced

100g cherry tomatoes, halved

20g red onions, sliced

50g rocket salad

5g celery leaves

150g salmon fillet without skin

2 teaspoons of brown sugar

1 chicory, halved lengthwise

Preheat oven to 425 °.

The dressing: Mix parsley, lemon juice, capers and 2 teaspoons of olive oil in a blender to a sauce.

Mix avocado, tomato, red onion and celery green for the salad. Rub the salmon with a little oil and fry it briefly on both sides in a coated pan. Then place in the oven for about five minutes.

Mix 1 teaspoon of olive oil with the brown sugar and rub it into the cut surfaces of the chicory. Fry on medium heat for 3 minutes in a pan.

Mix the salad with the dressing and serve with salmon and chicory.

Turkey meatball skewers

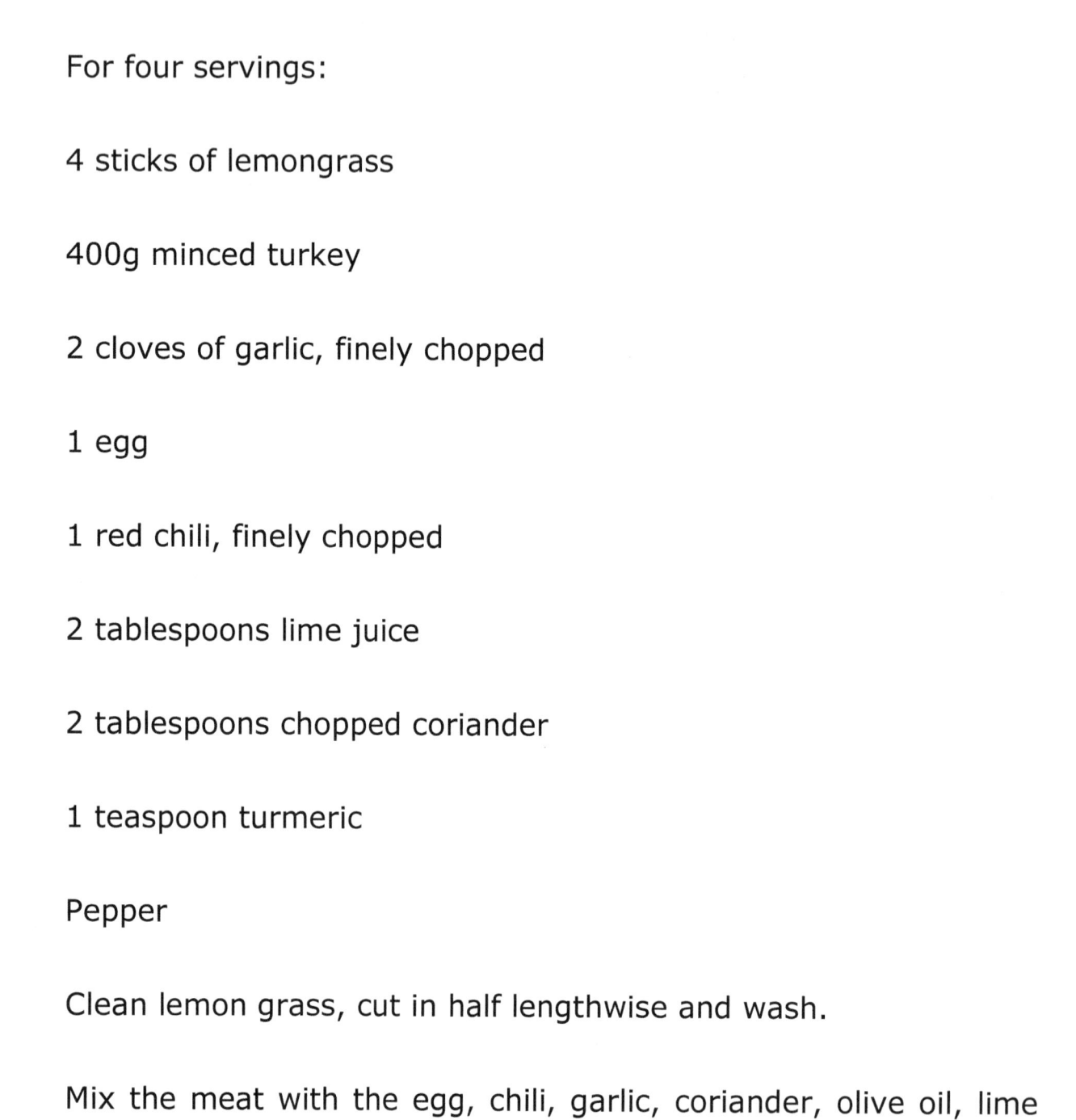

For four servings:

4 sticks of lemongrass

400g minced turkey

2 cloves of garlic, finely chopped

1 egg

1 red chili, finely chopped

2 tablespoons lime juice

2 tablespoons chopped coriander

1 teaspoon turmeric

Pepper

Clean lemon grass, cut in half lengthwise and wash.

Mix the meat with the egg, chili, garlic, coriander, olive oil, lime juice, turmeric and a little pepper. Make little balls out of them.

Put the balls on the lemongrass skewer and grill them as you like. Cook them in the oven or fry them in the pan until the balls are ready. A small salad goes with it.

Cod with vegetables

For one serving:

20g miso

1 tablespoon of mirin

2 tablespoons of olive oil

40g celery, sliced

1 garlic clove finely chopped

200g cod fillet without skin

1 chili, finely chopped

1 teaspoon finely chopped ginger

60g green beans

20g red onion, sliced

50g kale, coarsely chopped

30g buckwheat

1 teaspoon turmeric

1 teaspoon sesame seeds

5g parsley, roughly chopped

1 tablespoon soy sauce

Mix miso, mirin and a tablespoon of oil. Marinate the cod for at least 30 minutes.

Preheat the oven to 425 ° and then bake the cod for 10 minutes.

In the meantime, heat the remaining oil in a large frying pan. Sauté the onion in it, then add the celery, garlic, chili, ginger, green beans and kale. Fry until the kale is done. If necessary, add some water to facilitate the cooking process.

Boil buckwheat with the turmeric according to the instructions in the package.

When the buckwheat is ready, add sesame, parsley and soy sauce to the vegetables and serve the buckwheat with vegetables and fish.

Mushroom Courgetti & Lemon Caper Pesto

Ingredients

4 courgettes (zucchinis)

10 oyster mushrooms, sliced

1 red onion, sliced

2 tablespoons olive oil

2 tablespoons lemon caper pesto (see recipe)

50g (2oz) rocket (arugula) leaves

Serves 4

127 calories per serving

Directions:

Spiralize the courgettes into spaghetti. If you don't have a spiralizer, finely cut the vegetables lengthways into long 'spaghetti' strips. Heat the olive oil in a frying pan, add the mushrooms and onions and cook for minutes. Add in the courgettes and the pesto and cook for 5 minutes. Scatter the rocket (arugula) leaves onto plates and serve the courgettes on top.

Chicken Stir-Fry

Ingredients

150g (5oz) egg noodles

50g (2oz) cauliflower florets, roughly chopped

25g (1oz) kale, finely chopped

25g (1oz) mange tout

2 sticks of celery, finely chopped

2 chicken breasts

1 red pepper (bell pepper), chopped

1 clove of garlic

2 tablespoons soy sauce

100mls (3½ fl oz) chicken stock (broth)

1 tablespoon olive oil

Serves 2

566 calories per serving

Directions:

Cook the noodles according to the instructions then set aside and keep warm. Heat the oil in a wok or frying pan and add in the garlic and chicken. Add in the kale, celery, cauliflower, red pepper (bell pepper), mange tout and cook for 4 minutes. Pour in the chicken stock (broth) and soy sauce and cook for 3 minutes or until the chicken is thoroughly cooked. Stir in the cooked noodles and serve.

Tuna With Lemon Herb Dressing

Ingredients

4 tuna steaks

1 tablespoon olive oil

For the dressing:

25g (1oz) pitted green olives, chopped

2 tablespoons fresh parsley, chopped

1 tablespoon fresh basil, chopped

2 tablespoons olive oil

Freshly squeezed juice of 1 lemon

Serves 4

241 calories per serving

Directions:

Heat a tablespoon of olive oil in a griddle pan. Add the tuna steaks and cook on a high heat for 2-3 minutes on each side. Reduce the cooking time if you want them rare. Place the **Ingredients** for the dressing into a bowl and combine them well. Serve the tuna steaks with a dollop of dressing over them. Serve alongside a leafy rocket salad.

Kale, Apple & Fennel Soup

Ingredients

450g (1lb) kale, chopped

200g (7oz) fennel, chopped

2 apples, peeled, cored and chopped

2 tablespoons fresh parsley, chopped

1 tablespoon olive oil

Sea salt

Freshly ground black pepper

Serves 4

99 calories per serving

Directions:

Heat the oil in a saucepan, add the kale and fennel and cook for 5 minutes until the fennel has softened. Stir in the apples and parsley. Cover with hot water, bring it to the boil and simmer for

10 minutes. Using a hand blender or food processor blitz until the soup is smooth. Season with salt and pepper.

Lentil Soup

Ingredients

175g (6oz) red lentils

1 red onion, chopped

1 clove of garlic, chopped

2 sticks of celery, chopped

2 carrots, chopped

½ bird's-eye chilli

1 teaspoon ground cumin

1 teaspoon ground turmeric

1 teaspoon ground coriander (cilantro)

1200mls (2 pints) vegetable stock (broth)

2 tablespoons olive oil

Sea salt

Freshly ground black pepper

Serves 4

147 calories per serving

Directions:

Heat the oil in a saucepan and add the onion and cook for 5 minutes. Add in the carrots, lentils, celery, chilli, coriander (cilantro), cumin, turmeric and garlic and cook for 5 minutes. Pour in the stock (broth), bring it to the boil, reduce the heat and simmer for 45 minutes. Using a hand blender or food processor, puree the soup until smooth. Season with salt and pepper. Serve.

Cauliflower & Walnut Soup

Ingredients

450g (1lb) cauliflower, chopped

8 walnut halves, chopped

1 red onion, chopped

900mls (1½ pints) vegetable stock (broth)

100mls (3½ fl oz) double cream (heavy cream)

½ teaspoon turmeric

1 tablespoon olive oil

Serves 4

249 calories per serving

Directions:

Heat the oil in a saucepan, add the cauliflower and red onion and cook for 4 minutes, stirring continuously. Pour in the stock (broth), bring to the boil and cook for 15 minutes. Stir in the walnuts, double cream and turmeric. Using a food processor or hand blender, process the soup until smooth and creamy. Serve into bowls and top off with a sprinkling of chopped walnuts.

Celery & Blue Cheese Soup

Ingredients

125g (4oz) blue cheese

25g (1oz) butter

1 head of celery (approx 650g)

1 red onion, chopped

900mls (1½ pints) chicken stock (broth)

150mls (5fl oz) single cream

Serves 4

312 calories per serving

Directions:

Heat the butter in a saucepan, add the onion and celery and cook until the vegetables have softened. Pour in the stock, bring to the boil then reduce the heat and simmer for 15 minutes. Pour in the cream and stir in the cheese until it has melted. Serve and eat straight away.

Spicy Squash Soup

Ingredients

150g (5oz) kale

1 butternut squash, peeled, de-seeded and chopped

1 red onion, chopped

3 bird's-eye chillies, chopped

3 cloves of garlic

2 teaspoons turmeric

1 teaspoon ground ginger

600mls (1 pint) vegetable stock (broth)

2 tablespoons olive oil

Serves 4

128 calories per serving

Directions:

Heat the olive oil in a saucepan, add the chopped butternut squash and onion and cook for 6 minutes until softened. Stir in the kale, garlic, chilli, turmeric and ginger and cook for 2 minutes, stirring constantly. Pour in the vegetable stock (broth) bring it to the boil and cook for 20 minutes. Using a food processor or a hand blender process until smooth. Serve on its own or with a swirl of cream or crème fraiche. Enjoy.

French Onion Soup

Ingredients

750g (1¾ lbs) red onions, thinly sliced

50g (2oz) Cheddar cheese, grated (shredded)

12g (½ oz) butter

2 teaspoons flour

2 slices wholemeal bread

900mls (1½ pints) beef stock (broth)

1 tablespoon olive oil

Serves 4

228 calories per serving

Directions:

Heat the butter and oil in a large pan. Add the onions and gently cook on a low heat for 25 minutes, stirring occasionally. Add in the flour and stir well. Pour in the stock (broth) and keep stirring. Bring to the boil, reduce the heat and simmer for 30 minutes.

Cut the slices of bread into triangles, sprinkle with cheese and place them under a hot grill (broiler) until the cheese has melted. Serve the soup into bowls and add 2 triangles of cheesy toast on top. Enjoy.

Chapter 4: Salads

Kale and Beef salad

Ingredients

250g (9oz) kale, finely chopped

50g (2oz) walnuts, chopped

75g (3oz) beef, crumbled

1 apple, peeled, cored and sliced

4 medjool dates, chopped

For the Dressing

75g (3oz) cranberries

½ red onion, chopped

3 tablespoons olive oil

3 tablespoons water

2 teaspoons honey

1 tablespoon red wine vinegar

Sea salt

Serves 4

342 calories per serving

Method

Place the **Ingredients** for the dressing into a food processor and process until smooth. If it seems too thick you can add a little extra water if necessary. Place all the **Ingredients** for the salad into a bowl. Pour on the dressing and toss the salad until it is well coated in the mixture.

Arugula salad

Ingredients

75g (3oz) fresh rocket (arugula) leaves

100g (3½ oz) strawberries, halved

8 walnut halves

2 tablespoons flaxseeds

Serves 2

268 calories per serving

Directions:

Combine all the **Ingredients** in a bowl then scatter them onto two plates. For an extra Sirt food boost you can drizzle over some olive oil.

Tuna, Tomato and Eggs Salad

100g red chicory

150g tuna flakes in brine, drained

100g cucumber

25g rocket

6 kalamata olives, pitted

2 hard-boiled eggs, peeled and quartered

2 tomatoes, chopped

2 tbsp fresh parsley, chopped

1 red onion, chopped

1 celery stalk

1 tbsp capers

2 tbsp garlic vinaigrette

Instructions

Combine all **Ingredients** in a bowl and serve.

Crude Brownie Bites

All out Time: 5 minutes

Serves: 6

Ingredients:

2½ cups entire walnuts

¼ cup almonds

2½ cups Medjool dates

1 cup cacao powder

1 teaspoon vanilla concentrate

⅛-¼ teaspoon ocean salt

Steps:

Spot everything in a nourishment processor until very much joined.

Fold into balls and spot on a heating sheet and freeze for 30 minutes or refrigerate for 2 hours.

Potato Salad

Potato Salad - New Sirtfood Recipes

Ingredients: (serves 2)

200g celery, generally slashed

100g apple, generally slashed

50g walnuts, generally slashed

1 little red onion, generally slashed

1 head of chicory, slashed

10g level parsley, slashed

1 tbsp escapades

10g lovage or celery leaves, generally slashed

For the dressing:

1 tbsp additional virgin olive oil

1 tsp balsamic vinegar

1 teaspoon Dijon mustard

Juice of a large portion of a lemon

Blend the celery, apple, walnuts, onion, parsley, escapades and lavage/celery in a medium-sized plate of mixed greens bowl and blend. Make the dressing by whisking together the oil, vinegar, mustard and lemon juice. Drizzle over the plate of mixed greens, blend and serve!

Chargrilled Beef

Ingredients:

100g potatoes, stripped and cut into 2cm bones

1 tbsp additional virgin olive oil

5g parsley, finely hacked

50g red onion, cut into rings

50g kale, cut

1 garlic clove, finely hacked

120–150g x 3.5cm-thick meat filet steak or 2cm-thick sirloin steak

40ml red wine

150ml meat stock

1 tsp tomato purée

1 tsp cornflour, broke up in 1 tbsp water

Instructions:

Heat the oven to 220ºC/gas 7.

Spot the potatoes in a pot of boiling water, take back to the boil and cook for 4–5 minutes, at that point channel. Spot in a simmering tin with 1 teaspoon of the oil and dish in the hot stove for 35–45 minutes. Turn the potatoes like clockwork to guarantee in any event, cooking. At the point when cooked, expel from the oven, sprinkle with the hacked parsley and blend well.

Fry the onion in 1 teaspoon of the oil over a medium heat for 5–7 minutes, until delicate and pleasantly caramelized. Keep warm. Steam the kale for 2–3 minutes at that point channel. Fry the garlic tenderly in ½ teaspoon of oil for 1 moment, until delicate yet not shaded. Include the kale and fry for a further 1–2 minutes, until delicate. Keep warm.

Heat an ovenproof skillet over a high heat until smoking. Coat the meat in ½ a teaspoon of the oil and fry in the hot skillet over a medium–high heat as indicated by how you like your meat done. If you like your meat medium it is smarter to burn the meat and afterward move the container to a stove set at 220ºC/gas 7 and finish the cooking that path for the endorsed occasions.

Expel the meat from the dish and put aside to rest. Add the wine to the hot skillet to raise any meat buildup. Air pocket to lessen the wine considerably, until syrupy and with a concentrated flavor.

Include the stock and tomato purée to the steak container and bring to the boil, at that point add the corn flour glue to thicken your sauce, including it a little at once until you have your ideal consistency. Mix in any of the juices from the refreshed steak and present with the broiled potatoes, kale, onion rings and red wine sauce.

New Saag Paneer

279 calories

3 of your SIRT 5 per day

Serves 2 • Ready in a short time

2 tsp rapeseed oil

200g paneer.

Cut into 3D shapes

Salt and crisply ground dark pepper

1 red onion, cleaved

1 little thumb (3 cm) new ginger, stripped and cut into matchsticks

1 clove garlic, stripped and daintily cut

1 green bean stew, deseeded and finely cut

100g cherry tomatoes, split

1/2 tsp ground coriander

1/2 tsp ground cumin

1/4 tsp ground turmeric

1/2 tsp gentle stew powder

1/2 tsp salt

100g new spinach leaves

Little bunch (10g) parsley, cleaved

Little bunch (10g) coriander, cleaved

Heat the oil in a wide lidded skillet over a high heat. Season the paneer liberally with salt and pepper and hurl into the dish. Fry for a couple of moments until brilliant, blending regularly. Expel from the dish with an opened spoon and put in a safe spot.

Reduce the heat and include the onion. Fry for 5 minutes before including the ginger, garlic and stew. Cook for another couple of minutes before including the cherry tomatoes. Put the top on the dish and cook for a further 5 minutes.

Add the flavors and salt, at that point mix. Return the paneer to the dish and mix until covered. Add the spinach to the container together with the parsley and coriander and put the cover on. Permit the spinach to shrivel for 1-2 minutes, at that point consolidate into the dish. Serve right away.

Mocha Chocolate Mousse

Everybody appreciates chocolate mousse and this one has a brilliant light and breezy surface. It is brisk and simple to make and is best served the day after it's made.

Serves 4-6

Ingredients:

250g dim chocolate (85% cocoa solids)

6 medium unfenced eggs, isolated

4 tbsp solid dark espresso

4 tbsp almond milk

Chocolate espresso beans, to enrich

Steps:

1. Soften the chocolate in a huge bowl set over a skillet of delicately stewing water, ensuring the base of the bowl doesn't contact the water. Expel the bowl from the heat and leave the dissolved chocolate to cool to room temperature.

2. When the softened chocolate is at room temperature, race in the egg yolks each in turn and afterward tenderly overlap in the espresso and almond milk.

3. utilizing a hand-held electric blender, whisk the egg whites until firm pinnacles structure, at that point blend several tablespoons into the chocolate blend to release it. Delicately overlap in the rest of, an enormous metal spoon.

4. Move the mousse to singular glasses and smooth the surface. Spread with stick film and chill for in any event 2 hours, preferably medium-term. Enliven with chocolate espresso beans before serving.

Buckwheat Superfood Muesli

Ingredients:

20g buckwheat pieces

10g buckwheat puffs

15g coconut pieces or parched coconut

40g Medjool dates, hollowed and cleaved

15g walnuts, cleaved

10g cocoa nibs

100g strawberries, hulled and cleaved

100g plain Greek yogurt (or veggie lover elective, for example, soy or coconut yogurt)

Instructions

Blend the entirety of the above **Ingredients**: together (forget about the strawberries and yogurt if not serving straight away).

NOTES

In the event that you need to make this in mass or set it up the prior night, just join the dry **Ingredients**: and store it in an impermeable holder. All you have to do the following day is include the strawberries and yogurt and it is all set.

Exquisite Turmeric Pancakes with Lemon Yogurt Sauce

Serves: 8 hotcakes

Ingredients:

For The Yogurt Sauce

1 cup plain Greek yogurt

1 garlic clove, minced

1 to 2 tablespoons lemon juice (from 1 lemon), to taste

¼ teaspoon ground turmeric

10 crisp mint leaves, minced

2 teaspoons lemon pizzazz (from 1 lemon)

For The Pancakes

2 teaspoons ground turmeric

1½ teaspoons ground cumin

1 teaspoon salt

1 teaspoon ground coriander

½ teaspoon garlic powder

½ teaspoon naturally ground dark pepper

1 head broccoli, cut into florets

3 enormous eggs, gently beaten

2 tablespoons plain unsweetened almond milk

1 cup almond flour

4 teaspoons coconut oil

Steps:

1. Make the yogurt sauce. Taste and enjoy with more lemon juice, if possible. Keep in a safe spot or freeze until prepared to serve.

3. Spot the broccoli in a nourishment processor, and heartbeat until the florets are separated into little pieces. Move the broccoli to an enormous bowl and include the eggs, almond milk, and almond flour. Mix in the flavor blend and consolidate well.

4. Heat 1 teaspoon of the coconut oil in a nonstick dish over medium-low heat. Empty ¼ cup player into the skillet. Cook the

hotcake until little air pockets start to show up superficially and the base is brilliant darker, 2 to 3 minutes. Flip over and cook the hotcake for 2 to 3 minutes more. To keep warm, move the cooked hotcakes to a stove safe dish and spot in a 200°F oven.

5. Keep making the staying 3 hotcakes, utilizing the rest of the oil and player.

Sirt Chili Con Carne

Serves 4

1 red onion, finely cleaved

3 garlic cloves, finely cleaved

2 10,000 foot chillies, finely hacked

1 tbsp additional virgin olive oil

1 tbsp ground cumin

1 tbsp ground turmeric

400g lean minced hamburger (5 percent fat)

150ml red wine

1 red pepper, cored, seeds evacuated and cut into reduced down pieces

2 x 400g tins cleaved tomatoes

1 tbsp tomato purée

1 tbsp cocoa powder

150g tinned kidney beans

300ml hamburger stock

5g coriander, cleaved

5g parsley, cleaved

160g buckwheat

In a meal, fry the onion, garlic and bean stew in the oil over a medium heat for 2-3 minutes, at that point include the flavors and cook for a moment.

Include the minced hamburger and dark colored over a high heat. Include the red wine and permit it to rise to decrease it considerably.

You may need to add a little water to accomplish a thick, clingy consistency. Just before serving, mix in the hacked herbs.

In the interim, cook the buckwheat as indicated by the bundle guidelines and present with the stew.

Chickpea, Quinoa and Turmeric Curry Recipe

Serves 6

Ingredients:

500g new potatoes, split

3 garlic cloves, squashed

3 teaspoons ground turmeric

1 teaspoon ground coriander

1 teaspoon stew drops or powder

1 teaspoon ground ginger

400g container of coconut milk

1 tbsp tomato purée

400g container of slashed tomatoes

Salt and pepper

180g quinoa

400g container of chickpeas, depleted and flushed

150g spinach

Techniques:

Spot the potatoes in a dish of cold water and bring to the boil, at that point let them cook for around 25 minutes until you can undoubtedly stick a blade through them. Channel them well.

Spot the potatoes in an enormous skillet and include the garlic, turmeric, coriander, bean stew, ginger, coconut milk, tomato purée and tomatoes. Bring to the boil, season with salt and pepper, at that point include the quinoa with a cup of simply boil water (300ml).

Diminish the heat to a stew, place the top on and permit to cook. Throughout the following 30 minutes, blending at regular intervals or so to ensure nothing adheres to the base. (This is a significant long cooking time, yet this is to what extent quinoa takes to cook in every one of these **Ingredients**:, as opposed to simply in water.) Halfway through cooking, include the chickpeas. When there are only 5 minutes left, include the spinach and mix it in until it withers. Once the quinoa has cooked and is cushioned, not crunchy, it's prepared.

On the off chance that you like a touch of heat, add a cut red bean stew to the cooking curry simultaneously as different flavors

Chapter 5: Snacks

Kale chips

Ingredients:

1 large head of curly kale, wash, dry and pulled from stem 1 tbsp. extra virgin olive oil

Minced parsley

Squeeze of lemon juice

Cayenne pepper (just a pinch)

Dash of soy sauce

Instructions:

In a large bowl, rip the kale from the stem into palm sized pieces. Sprinkle the minced parsley, olive oil, soy sauce, a squeeze of the lemon juice and a very small pinch of the cayenne powder. Toss with a set if tongs or salad forks, and make sure to coat all of the leaves.

If you have a dehydrator, turn it on to 118 F, spread out the kale on a dehydrator sheet, and leave in there for about 2 hours.

If you are cooking them, place parchment paper on top of a cookie sheet. Lay the bed of kale and separate it a bit to make sure the kale is evenly toasted. Cook for 10-15 minutes maximum at 250F.

Honey nuts

Ingredients

150g (5oz) walnuts

150g (5oz) pecan nuts

50g (2oz) softened butter

1 tablespoon honey

½ bird's-eye chilli, very finely chopped and de-seeded

Makes 20 servings 126 calories per serving

Method

Preheat the oven to 180C/360F. Combine the butter, honey and chilli in a bowl then add the nuts and stir them well. Spread the nuts onto a lined baking sheet and roast them in the oven for 10 minutes, stirring once halfway through. Remove from the oven and allow them to cool before eating.

Tofu guacamole

Ingredients

225g (8oz) silken tofu

3 avocados

2 tablespoon fresh coriander (cilantro) chopped

1 bird's-eye chilli

Juice of 1 lime

Serves 6

162 calories per serving

Method

Place all of the **Ingredients** into a food processor and blend a soft chunky consistency. Serve with crudités.

Watermelon Juice

Serves 1

Ingredients

20g of young kale leaves

250g of watermelon chunks

4 mint leaves

½ cucumber

Instructions

1. Remove the stalks from the kale and roughly chop it.

2. Peel the cucumber, if preferred, and then halve it and seed it.

3. Place all **Ingredients** in a blender or juicer and process until you achieve a desired consistency. Serve immediately.

Snack bites

120g walnuts

30g dark chocolate (85% cocoa)

250g dates

1 tablespoon pure cocoa powder

1 tablespoon turmeric

1 tablespoon of olive oil

Contents of a vanilla pod or some vanilla flavoring

Coarsely crumble the chocolate and mix it with the walnuts in a food processor into a fine powder.

Then add the other **Ingredients** and stir until you have a uniform dough. If necessary, add 1 to 2 tablespoons of water.

Form 15 pieces from the mixture and refrigerate in an airtight tin for at least one hour.

The bites will remain in the refrigerator for a week.

Choc Bites

Makes 15-20 bites

Ingredients

1-2 tablespoons of water

1 tablespoon of extra-virgin olive oil

1 tablespoon of ground turmeric

250g of Medjool dates- pitted

1 tablespoon of vanilla extract or scraped seeds of 1 vanilla pod

30g dark of chocolate (85% cocoa solids) broken into pieces or cocoa nibs

120g of walnuts

1 tablespoon of cocoa powder

Instructions

1. Place the chocolate and walnuts in a food processor and run it until you get a fine powder. Add the other **Ingredients** (except water) and process until a ball forms.

2. Depending on its consistency, you may, or may not need to add water (we don't want it to be too sticky).

3. Form bite-sized balls and place them in the refrigerator in an airtight container for about an hour before serving. You could roll the balls in some desiccated coconut or cocoa if desired. They will keep in the fridge for about a week.

Berries Banana Smoothie

Serves 2

Ingredients

½ cup of coconut milk

1½ cups of mixed berries (strawberries and blueberries)- could be frozen or fresh

¾ cup of water

4 ice cubes

1 tablespoon of molasses

1 banana

Instructions

1. Place all the **Ingredients** in a blender and blend until smooth.

2. You can add water to the smoothie until you achieve your desired consistency then serve.

Grape and Melon Smoothie

Serves 1

Ingredients

100g of cantaloupe melon

100g of red seedless grapes

30g of young spinach leaves, stalks removed

½ cucumber

Instructions

1. Peel the cucumber, then cut it into half. Remove the seeds and chop it roughly.

2. Peel the cantaloupe, deseed it, and cut it into chunks.

3. Place all **Ingredients** in a blender and blend until smooth.

Green Tea Smoothie

Serves 1

Ingredients

2 teaspoons of honey

250ml of milk

2 teaspoons of matcha green tea powder

6 ice cubes

½ teaspoon of vanilla bean paste (not extract) or a scrape of the seeds from vanilla pod

2 ripe bananas

Instructions

1. Place all the **Ingredients** in a blender and run until you achieve a desired consistency.

2. Serve into two glasses and enjoy.

Chapter 6: Juice and Cocktails

Sirtfood green juice

Ingredients:

2 large handfuls kale

5 grams of parsley

½ green apple

2–3 large stalks green celery plus the leaves

A large handful rocket (about 30 g)

Juice of ½ lemon

½ level tsp matcha green tea

A very small handful lovage leaves (optional)

Procedure:

Simply mix all the greens—rocket, parsley, kale and lovage using a juicer, just fully juice them. Your target is to juice around 50ml from the greens.

Next step is to add the green apple and the celery.

Simply squeeze the lemon into the juice. Most likely you will have more than 250ml of juice at this stage.

When ready to consume, pour into a glass and you can now add your matcha green tea powder. Stir and enjoy!

Berries juice

Ingredients

A cup of strawberries

A cup of blueberries

1 green apple

2 stalk parsley

5og celery

½ teaspoon of matcha green tea

½ lemon

Instructions

Wash the vegetables and fruits, blend. Also, add green tea leave to it

Squeeze the lemon juice into it

With a fine mesh, strain the juice if you want

Transfer to a cup and top with water if need be

Grapefruit blast

Ingredients

1 grapefruit, peeled

2 stalks of celery

50g (2oz) kale

½ teaspoon matcha powder

Serves 1

71 calories per serving

Method

Place all the **Ingredients** into a blender with enough water to cover them and blitz until smooth.

Blueberry blend

Dish out s 2 - Ready in 2 minutes.

Things needed.

1 ripe banana.

100g blueberries.

100g blackberries.

2 table spoon natural yogurt.

200ml milk.

Directions

Blend all the things required together until smooth.

Sirt Energy Balls

Yields 20 balls

Ingredients

1 mug of mixed nuts (with plenty of walnuts)

7 Medjool dates

1 tablespoon of coconut oil

2 tablespoons of cocoa powder

Zest of 1 orange (optional)

Instructions

1. Start by placing the nuts in a food processor and grind them until almost powdered (more or less depending on the preferred texture of your energy balls).

2. Add the Medjool dates, coconut oil, cacao powder, and run the blender again until fully mixed. Place the blend in a refrigerator for half an hour, and then shape them into balls. You can add in the zest of an orange as you blend.

Kale and Blackcurrant Smoothie

Serves 1

Ingredients

1 cup of freshly made green tea

2 teaspoon of honey

10 baby kale leaves with the stalks removed

1 ripe banana

40g of blackcurrants

6 ice cubes

Instructions

1. First wash, then stalk the blackcurrants and place them in a blender.

2. Pour the honey into the green tea until it fully dissolves, and then add this to the blender. Add the rest of the **Ingredients** and run the blender until you get a smooth mixture. Serve immediately.

Chapter 7: Desserts

Yogurt nuts and berries

Ingredients

100g (3½ oz) plain Greek yogurt

50g (2oz) berries, chopped

6 walnut halves, chopped

Sprinkling of cocoa powder

Serves 1

296 calories

Directions:

Stir half of the chopped berries into the yogurt. Using a glass, place a layer of yogurt with a sprinkling of berries and walnuts, followed by another layer of the same until you reach the top of the glass. Garnish with walnuts pieces and a dusting of cocoa powder.

Sirt muesli

Number of serving: 2

Prep time: Prepare at night against tomorrow.

Ingredients:

200g of strawberries, hulled and chopped

200g of plain Greek yogurt (soya or coconut yogurt for vegans)

30g of either coconut flakes or desiccated coconut

40g of buckwheat flakes

30g of walnuts, chopped

80g of Medjool dates, pitted and chopped

20g of cocoa nibs

20g of buckwheat puffs

Instructions

Place all the **Ingredients** in a container at night and mix apart from yogurt and strawberries. Allow staying till the next day.

Add the strawberries and yogurt and serve at once

Spiced poached apples

Ingredients

4 apples

2 tablespoons honey

4 star anise

2 cinnamon sticks

300mls (½ pint) green tea

Serves 4

99 calories per serving

Method

Place the honey and green tea into a saucepan and bring to the boil. Add the apples, star anise and cinnamon. Reduce the heat and simmer gently for 15 minutes. Serve the apples with a dollop of crème fraiche or Greek yogurt.

Sirt Chocolate brownies

Ingredients

200g (7oz) dark chocolate (min 85% cocoa)

200g (7oz) medjool dates, stone removed

100g (3½oz) walnuts, chopped

3 eggs

25mls (1fl oz) melted coconut oil

2 teaspoons vanilla essence

½ teaspoon baking soda

Makes 14 197 calories per serving

Method

Place the dates, chocolate, eggs, coconut oil, baking soda and vanilla essence into a food processor and mix until smooth. Stir the walnuts into the mixture. Pour the mixture into a shallow baking tray. Transfer to the oven and bake at 180C/350F for 25-30 minutes. Allow it to cool. Cut into pieces and serve.

Pistachio fudge

Ingredients

225g (8oz) medjool dates

100g (3½ oz) pistachio nuts, shelled (or other nuts)

50g (2oz) desiccated (shredded) coconut

25g (1oz) oats

2 tablespoons water

Serves 10

162 calories per serving

Method

Place the dates, nuts, coconut, oats and water into a food processor and process until the **Ingredients** are well mixed. Remove the mixture and roll it to 2cm (1 inch) thick. Cut it into 10 pieces and serve.

CONCLUSION

We have come to the end of the line. I'm happy and proud to have participated with you in this fantastic journey, and I hope that these tips and recipes have been very useful, especially for the beginners who are reading me.

I recommend you to keep following my publications and practice a lot to make and remake these delicious dishes.

Obviously I advise everyone, before doing any diet, to always talk to a specialized doctor and get the best follow up, so that you can always experience rich and tasty dishes.

Thank you very much and enjoy

CPSIA information can be obtained
at www.ICGtesting.com
Printed in the USA
BVHW092215230321
603261BV00014B/1087